How to Become a Successful Singer

by

Dame Clara Butt

Enrico Caruso

Ben Davies

Dame Nellie Melba

Double 9 BOOKS

How to Become a Successful Singer

by Dame Clara Butt, Enrico Caruso,
Ben Davies, Dame Nellie Melba

ISBN: 978-93-62206-95-4

Published by

DOUBLE 9 BOOKS
2/13-B, Ansari Road
Daryaganj, New Delhi – 110002
info@double9books.com
www.double9books.com
Tel. 011-40042856

ABOUT THE AUTHOR

"Dame Clara Butt, Enrico Caruso, Ben Davies, and Dame Nellie Melba share their expertise in 'How to Become a Successful Singer,' offering invaluable insights and techniques garnered from their illustrious careers. This masterpiece serves as a comprehensive guide for aspiring vocalists, covering everything from vocal technique and stage presence to the nuances of interpretation and artistic expression. With wisdom gleaned from years of experience on the world's most prestigious stages, these esteemed singers provide a roadmap for achieving excellence in the realm of vocal performance. Whether you're a budding soprano, a seasoned baritone, or somewhere in between, this book offers practical advice and inspiration to help you unlock your full potential as a singer. From mastering breath control to honing your phrasing and interpretation, each chapter is filled with actionable tips and exercises designed to enhance your vocal prowess and captivate audiences. 'How to Become a Successful Singer' is a must-read for anyone with a passion for singing and a desire to make their mark on the world stage."

CONTENTS

HOW TO BECOME A SUCCESSFUL SINGER. By MADAME CLARA BUTT 7

THE GIFT OF SONG WITH PRACTICAL ADVICE ON VOICE CULTURE By MADAME MELBA 16

HINTS ON THE CULTIVATION OF THE VOICE By ENRICO CARUSO 27

HOW TO ATTAIN SUCCESS IN SINGING By BEN DAVIES 33

HOW TO BECOME A SUCCESSFUL SINGER. By MADAME CLARA BUTT

The question of how to sing a song involves touching upon a variety of points that might not at first sight be associated with the subject. Four distinct factors play prominent parts in the singing of any song, however simple. These are the Voice, the Singer, the Master, and the Song.

Of these, of course, the voice is of primary importance; for unless an individual possesses in some degree the gift of song it is impossible for him or her to become a singer. In very many cases, needless to say, correct training, by showing how the vocal organs can be used to the best advantage, may achieve some sort of result. But the voice so produced is often of an artificial character, which can never approach the purely "natural" voice.

It is, I believe, held by a great many people that only those can sing who possess a throat and vocal organs suitable for the production of the voice, but my own views on the subject do not coincide with this idea at all. My point of view is that if you are meant to be a singer you will sing. "God sent His singers upon earth," etc.

One often hears of operations upon the throat being performed with the object of improving the voice, but here again I find myself in entire disagreement. I think that if one is born with a deformity of the throat, and has always sung easily with it, any attempt to interfere with, or alter, that deformity, may end in destroying the power of song altogether.

When I was at the Royal College of Music I was constantly being urged to have my tonsils cut. For a long time I held out against it, but at last consented. However, while I was actually seated in the operating chair, the doctor asked me to sing the vowel sound "E" on a high note, and remarked upon the way my tonsils contracted while I sang it. All at once I recalled the case of a girl I knew, with a true soprano voice, who had lost the ability to sing in tune after her tonsils had been cut. Might it not be the same in my own case? This decided me in an instant. I refused to let the operation be performed, and from that day to this have never allowed my throat to be interfered with surgically in any way. Yet I have had every sort of throat that a singer would wish to avoid without my voice being affected in the least! I started life, almost, with diphtheria, have suffered from adenoids, and have experienced several attacks of quinsy. Among myself and my three sisters, all of us being singers, my throat is the worst of the lot, and not in the least like a singer's throat. The sister whose voice most nearly resembles mine is the one whose throat is most like mine; and the sister who has a throat and vocal organs which are ideal from an anatomical point of view possesses a soprano voice which, though particularly sweet, is not strong!

One thing that I think exercises an enormous amount of influence upon the quality of voices is climate. Review the climatic conditions of the various countries, and you cannot help remarking upon the number of natural voices that are met with in Italy and in Australia, in both of which countries the climate is unusually fine. I believe that the brilliance of the Australian climate must be reckoned with very seriously in accounting for the peculiar brilliance which is a characteristic of Australian singing voices, while that Italy is a country of singers is well known to everybody. At the same time, climatic conditions do not seem to affect the speaking voice, which I imagine is more a question of language. I have always thought that the English speaking voice is the best of any. There is none of that nasal, sonorous accent about it which, for instance, makes the speaking voice of the ordinary Italian so unpleasant. I was never so struck with this quality in Italian speaking voices as upon one occasion when staying at an hotel in Venice, where there was a cafe almost beneath our windows. Even the beauties of Venice hardly compensated for the nerve-racking nasal chatter that continually floated up to us from below.

It goes without saying that the voice needs a great deal of training and care if it is to be brought to the best development, and one of the first faults that must be cured is in the taking, and use of, the breath. This must be done in an entirely different way from that usually employed when speaking. It would be impossible for me to deal fully in such an article as this with the question of how to take breath, and as it is one of the first lessons that a singing master should teach, I will confine myself here to saying that the main difference lies in the fact that, when speaking, the breath is usually taken from the chest, but that when singing it must be controlled by the abdominal muscles.

When singing, the muscles of the throat must be relaxed, and not contracted. Self-consciousness often does more to mar a good voice than anything else, since it leads to the contraction of the muscles. Have you never noticed how pleasantly some people sing or hum to themselves when they imagine they are not overheard, compared with the indifferent or even unpleasant manner in which they perform publicly? Here we have a direct example of the result of self-consciousness. Never mind your audience. Allow the song to carry you away, so that you sing easily and naturally.

To acquire perfect control over the throat muscles, so that they may be relaxed at will, is one of the most difficult points in voice training. And one of the most common mistakes made in this respect is in over-practice. The muscles of the throat are among the most delicate of the whole body, and I am convinced that it is a fatal error to overtax them, especially during the early training of the voice, by too much practice. Personally, my training was very gradual, and the greatest care was taken not to impose too much strain upon my throat at first. I am confident that a number of short practices of ten or fifteen minutes' duration, with intervals of rest between, are better than a few long periods, since the throat is thus less liable to become tired. Every expert in physical development will tell you that for the proper development of any set of muscles a gradual exercise that does not involve over-exertion is the best, and I would particularly emphasise the importance of this where the throat is concerned.

Another point in connection with the voice which is too often overlooked is the question of general health. My gardener sometimes complains that the flowers do not come to perfection owing to the poorness of the soil. The simile is a very good one. The vocal organs are like delicate flowers, capable of the best development when the soil in which they are planted—the body—is in perfect condition. It must be the object of all singers, therefore, to take the greatest care of their health.

Over-exercise of the body generally should also be avoided, just as much as over-exercising the throat. It is easier to sing when the rest of the body has not been over-tired. General exercise, though essential to health, can be overdone just as much as vocal exercise. These remarks apply particularly to the student. It is while the voice is being formed, more than after it has been formed, that it is likely to be affected by such considerations as those just mentioned.

The mind plays a prominent part where the voice is concerned. Worry, unhappiness, and mental strain of every description may lower the whole tone of the body, and, by lessening the inclination to sing, make singing more difficult. Unfortunately, one cannot take mental worries in small doses, but must put up with them as they come; and I only mention this to impress upon my readers the more forcibly how important the general health of mind and body is where the voice is concerned.

After all, the effect of mental or bodily strain upon the voice depends entirely upon the individual. Personally, whatever may be the state of my mind or my body, I am able to sing in a sort of subconscious state.

It would hardly be possible to hit upon a more striking illustration of what can be done when one is in a subconscious condition than what I am about to relate.

At one time and another I have had to have operations performed—for appendicitis, for instance—which have necessitated my being put under ether. On every single occasion I have sung in full voice while under the influence of the anæsthetic! This was most remarkable perhaps on the occasion when I was being operated upon for appendicitis, for then the abdominal muscles, which control one's breathing, must naturally have been interfered with.

The fact is that trouble, worry, and ill-health have no effect upon the voice itself. The voice is always there. It is only the power of using it that may be impaired.

As I have already pointed out, it is in the early stages of vocal training that the effects of ill-health, mental worry, or overwork are most likely to be felt. When the voice has been properly trained, and the vocal organs fully developed, they are less likely to suffer by the rest of the body being out of tune, and it is therefore of particular importance for beginners to bear my remarks in mind.

Here is another point which beginners should take to heart, and follow as far as they are able. Try to avoid over-anxiety. Students often make the mistake, through over-anxiety, of over-working their voices just before a concert, with the result that they are not at their best when on the platform. It is a good plan to rest both the body and the voice before singing in public.

I should like to emphasise the importance of this very fully. Young singers seem to lose sight, half the time, of the fact that they should be at their very best when on the platform. Personally I always keep, and have always kept, this clearly before my mind. It is the greatest possible mistake to waste your efforts at the last moment in private. Rest before you sing in public, in order that when you go on to the platform you may give your audience—who, after all, have paid to be entertained—of your best. Remember that while polishing is highly desirable, there is such a thing as over-polishing, and this, instead of improving, only wears out. I am a great believer in the quiet study of a song without the aid of a piano. Not only does this avoid tiring the voice, but it enables the singer to fully grasp all the beauty and the meaning of the words and the music, and so to enter into the spirit of the subject when upon the platform. When on tour I frequently adopt this method of studying. It enables one to be doing something useful when in the train, or elsewhere, when actual practice is undesirable or impracticable.

This resting of the voice before singing in public applies not only to vocal exercises, but to all kinds of over-exertion of the throat. Even those who are aware of the danger, and who are careful to refrain from singing-practice just before an appearance in public, very frequently forget that speaking may tire the voice every whit as much as singing. It is most important not to do too much talking for some hours before a public appearance is made. In this way the throat will be thoroughly rested.

In singing, as in everything else, experience teaches, better than any amount of instruction, what an individual is capable of, and how the full power and merit of the voice may best be acquired and preserved. When students have "found their feet" sufficiently to understand the best way to manage their voices, they will be able to regulate their practice according to what leads to the best result in each individual case. Some may be best suited by morning practice, others by afternoon practice. Personally, I put in most of my practice between the hours of eleven and one each morning.

The next factor to be considered is the Singer. Temperament, individuality, force, dramatic ability, perseverance, industry, keenness, and ambition all play a part in the making of a successful singer and in the singing of a song successfully. It is in the earlier stages of the singer's career that some of these qualities are most necessary, for many years of hard and constant study have sometimes to be faced. It is during this time that perseverance, industry, keenness, and ambition, if they are possessed, will help the student on so enormously; indeed, while ambition and keenness will do most perhaps in the early stages, industry and perseverance are required all the time, for it is impossible to reach a stage where there is nothing left to learn.

Singing is but one branch of art, and a singer can learn something from every other branch. From the Actor may be gleaned hints for dramatic effect; from the Painter may be acquired an appreciation of breadth and colour; from the Orator may be picked up many useful hints as regards enunciation, modulation, and emphasis; while the Writer may inspire those beautiful thoughts which, taking root in the singer's mind, help towards that mental health which is as important to the perfect voice as physical fitness. It will be seen, therefore, that one may never have done studying; for there are constantly new actors, new speakers, new painters, or new writers from whom something may be learnt, while in painting and literature alone there are great masterpieces to such number that no one singer could ever hope to study them all. It must be remembered, also, that what satisfied the public ten years ago does not satisfy them now, and as a singer must keep pace with every advancement that is made, there is constant study to be done.

The first thing the possessor of a voice looks out for is naturally some one to train it, and this brings us to the question of the master. It is not my intention to give advice as to the selection of master or masters; indeed, it would be impossible to do so, partly because there are so many masters between whom it would be invidious to make comparisons, and partly because such an article as this is intended more to assist the general run of students, who are spread over so large an area that they could not all reach the best-known masters, but are obliged to study locally. In England and in the Colonies there are many very good schools and colleges for vocal training, and there are competent teachers, most of them emanating from our great Colleges and Academies, within reach of almost every district. While I do not wish to appear unpatriotic, however, it must frankly be admitted that students must study on the Continent if the best results are to be achieved, since only on the Continent can they study in that "Musical Atmosphere" which is so essential a surrounding for one who essays an artistic career. Even if prolonged study on the Continent is out of the question, it is advisable, at all costs, for Continental musical centres to be visited. No musical education can otherwise be complete.

You must not think that I wish to run down English masters. Quite the contrary: I think you can get just as good masters here as abroad. It is simply the question of "Atmosphere"—surroundings. There is no city in England where the pupil can study amid such surroundings that music and artistic ideas and ideals hem him in on every side, so that they meet him whichever way he turns, and so that the feeling that music is the only thing in the world remains with him, waking and sleeping, during the whole period of his study.

Only when surrounded by such an Atmosphere can the student be properly developed where his musical ideas are concerned, for only these surroundings can develop that artistic temperament which is so essential.

And apart from the question of Musical Atmosphere, seeing that a singer is frequently called upon to render songs in French, German, and Italian, it is necessary that those languages should be studied in France, Germany, and Italy, if perfection is to be acquired.

It is a very grave fault of our musical colleges and academies that they employ, as a rule, English teachers to give instruction in foreign languages. If in one's student days one had a good master for these languages—a Frenchman to teach French, a German to teach German, and so on—it would be of the greatest possible assistance, and would save a considerable amount of time and labour, since so much less would have to be unlearned. It is not too much to say, I think, that our musical institutions will never reach the highest point of their utility till they do this.

But before learning to sing in foreign languages at all, it is essential that pupils should learn to sing in their own language. Masters in this country teach their pupils to sing passably in French, Italian, and German, but directly they attempt to sing in English one is horrified to find that their enunciation is so bad that it is impossible to understand the words they sing, and almost out of the question to tell what language they are singing in! Surely it should be the first object of the teacher to instruct his pupils in the singing of their own language.

I verily believe that the reason why our language is looked down upon for singing in is because so many of our native singers do not know how to sing it properly. There are much harder sounds in the German language, for instance. Yet German songs are constantly sung by singers of every nationality. How often does one hear of English songs being sung in France, Germany or Italy by French, German, and Italian singers? Even when they give recitals over here their programmes seldom include an English song, and one is even more struck by so many of our own vocalists giving recitals at which often not a single song in English is included!

When English is properly sung, it is as easy to sing in, and as beautiful to listen to, as any other language, and if students were taught how to sing it, its popularity among singers would, I feel convinced, quickly spread.

I remember very well indeed singing on one occasion to Madame Marchesi in Paris. I boldly chose an English song, and upon coming to the end of it, was much pleased by the tribute Madame Marchesi paid to our language when she said to me, "English is beautiful when sung like that!"

It should emphatically be the first duty of a master to teach his pupils how to use their native language, and no other should be attempted till they can do this perfectly. The slipshod methods so frequently met with now would then soon disappear, and I am sure it would not be long before other countries began to appreciate the many beauties of the English language for singing in, and we should get more songs written by good composers to some of our beautiful English poetry.

Before I leave this question of the master there is one other point for me to touch upon. Although, when once they have mastered the singing of their own language, pupils should seek the Musical Atmosphere of the Continent, it must be remembered that there is one branch of music which is peculiarly our own, and which must accordingly be studied here. I refer to Oratorio. England is the home of Oratorio, and consequently this style of singing cannot be studied abroad. And for any singer who looks forward to entering the musical profession, careful study of this branch is absolutely indispensable. Oratorio is very popular here, and English audiences will not for a moment tolerate singers who fail to acquit themselves well when they undertake it; and as most professionals have to do Oratorio work at one time or another, care must be taken that the public are not given renderings which fail through lack of proper study and application.

Oratorio entails much study and research that is unnecessary where other branches of singing are concerned. Not only must the whole work be studied so that the singer may become acquainted with the full intention of the composer, but a special study must be made of the character which the singer is to perform, in order that all the feelings and emotions he or she would have felt in real life may be properly understood before an attempt is made to reproduce them. If the best results are to be achieved, the life, habits, failings, aims, and ambitions of the character to be interpreted must, as far as possible, be carefully studied and thought about, in order that the singer may better appreciate the situations which occur, and know how the character portrayed would have felt and acted in them. The Bible throws considerable light upon the life and character of most of the personages who have a place in Oratorio, and it is therefore useful, when studying some particular work, to examine carefully that portion of the Bible which may throw light upon the subject.

Lastly, we come to the song, and this is a question upon which I hold very decided views. The object of singers should be to give the greatest amount of pleasure to their audiences, as well as to use all that is best and highest in their art to inspire good thoughts, and raise the mental standard of their hearers. The larger proportion of every audience can only follow the words of the song in English. They can fully appreciate the beauty of the music, I admit, and for this reason every artist should have some of the most beautiful songs of other countries in his or her repertoire, but it is a lamentable fact that good translations are very rare. I like to choose as many songs as possible in English, so that their meaning and their message can be readily understood and appreciated by my audience.

I believe that it is within the power of an artist to actually lessen, or, at any rate, to temporarily relieve, the cares and worries of which each member of an audience has a share; and I am sure that the easiest way to do so is to sing songs whose meaning, and whose message, is immediately understandable.

In conclusion, I cannot insist too strongly upon the necessity for hard work and perseverance for those who are to succeed in the world of music. Too many people imagine that the "gift" is everything. But, indeed, this is not the case, for though the "gift" is, of course, indispensable, much application and hard work are necessary before it can be made use of to the best advantage. Given a voice and some dramatic instinct, there still remains careful and laborious training to be gone through before a singer can know how to sing a song and be able to put that knowledge into practice. The great thing is to be sincere, to be individual, and to grasp at the beginning of one's career the impossibility of pleasing everybody, *and the necessity of being true to oneself,* and if others see the truth differently, be deferential, and not servile, to their alien point of view.

THE GIFT OF SONG WITH PRACTICAL ADVICE ON VOICE CULTURE By MADAME MELBA

During the years immediately preceding my first and, for me, my most memorable visit to Europe, the late Marquis of Normanby was Governor of Victoria. At that time I was regarded in Melbourne as a very good amateur pianist, much in request for private parties, at which I always played, and on very rare occasions also sang. At one of these functions, given at Government House, I gave some songs between the pianoforte selections, and the Marchioness of Normanby, in thanking me, said, "Child, some day you will give up the piano for singing, and then you will become famous."

That was the simple comment that set me seriously thinking of a career as a singer. I had always felt that I would become a professional in music—pianist, organist, violinist, perhaps, but something in music, at any rate; but from that moment I knew in an irresistible way that I was to be a singer.

That remark of the Marchioness made me understand, and determined me to grasp "the skirts of happy chance." I courted every semblance of opportunity, and I see now, as then, how fateful a factor opportunity must be with all who aim at a public career. Even the born singer may waste divine gifts for want of opportunity, and the possessor of highly developed vocal talent may entirely sink into obscurity without it.

Among students of similar talent and health she who succeeds is the one with alert mind, who is ever on the *qui vive* for her chance. The girl who fails is generally lacking in mental and physical energy—too prone to believe that opportunity on ready foot trips unsought even to the laggard's door. The born or inspired singer always sings, although in isolated cases want of opportunity may limit the sphere of those rarely endowed people.

While it is true that the present time offers extraordinary scope for art by reason of a wide-spread knowledge on all subjects, I think the increased chances of success which the growing popularity of music offers have been largely discounted by the numbers of performers and professors who, without proper qualifications have set themselves up as apostles of music, and unfairly and recklessly overcrowded a profession which should be exceptionally difficult to enter.

No doubt many aspirants—I speak solely of women—are encouraged and flattered by the fact that in the profession of music women fare better than in any other walk of life, and the monetary reward of great singers and teachers may be said to have reached a stage of almost extravagant appreciation.

In my opinion the great singers of our day would not be so few if there were more competent teachers and a more complete realisation of the greatness of the task. It is not that lovely voices are rarer than formerly, or talent more sparingly given of God. The piano or violin student will devote ten years to the technique of his instrument, while the vocalist or the teacher too often regards research at an end after studying a year or two, or even a few months only.

Just here, however, I should like to make it plain that the student who cannot give a promising account of herself after eighteen months' thorough study is, to my mind, never likely to do really great things. I do not mean for a moment that she should then be a full-fledged singer, but that she should be able to give clear indications as to future possibilities.

The real study actually begins after one has come before the public, and it is to subsequent development that the most earnest attention should be paid. Year after year the artiste will make striking progress if music be really in her soul, and from life and its varied experiences she will learn interpretative nuances which no other teacher can bestow. Let me say, too, that in this life-long study the singer must not be too rigidly bound by the tenets of technique. She must think and feel for herself, and to a great extent be guided by her individuality.

In too many cases the vocal student has only the merest smattering of knowledge about the marvellous and delicate mechanism that produces the singing voice. Languages and travel, too, are neglected for one reason or another, chiefly through the spirit of haste, the desire to reach ends by short cuts such as were unknown to the old Italian masters, who taught on physiological principles that were, on the whole, marvellously accurate; although in many respects we have greatly progressed since their day.

In every country with which I am familiar—and they are many—I have been struck by the voices maimed or entirely ruined by ignorant tuition. Of course it is not possible for me to hear more than a few of the students who seek my opinion on their voices, for I frequently have thirty or forty such applications in a single day; but almost without exception I find those I can hear following methods which are causing positive injury to the delicate vocal chords.

In all learned and mechanical professions certain technical tests are insisted on before a person is accepted as an authority; but in music it is not so. Any charlatan, whose only qualifications may be confidence and casual observation, may set up as a teacher and persistently trick the public, which is only too easily deceived. I speak strongly on this subject, having in mind the cruel vocal havoc to which I have just referred. Just as the engineer must know the structure and parts of his engine, or the architect the nature and relative values of material as well as the principles of design, so must the would-be singer understand the easily injured structure and delicate functions of voice mechanism.

A knowledge of the structure of the larynx, and the general muscular mechanism of voice-production, unequalled in delicacy anywhere in the human body save perhaps in eye and ear, will be a revelation, a very helpful revelation, to the student. And unless the structure of the larynx be understood, the "attack," or application of the air blast to the vocal strands, cannot be perfect.

If the student seeks the best, she must get a complete understanding of the methods of the old Italian masters, as sculptors turn to the Greek for what is soundest and noblest in the plastic art. Together with this recommendation, I join my condemnation of the tremolo and "white" voice so dear to many Italian singers.

I cannot too forcibly insist that the mere possession of a lovely voice is only the basis of vocal art. Nature occasionally startles one by the prodigality of her gifts, but no student has any right to expect to sing by inspiration, any more than an athlete may expect to win a race because he is naturally fleet of foot.

Methods of breathing, "attack," and the use of the registers must all be perfectly understood by the successful singer, who should likewise be complete master of all details relating to the structure and use of those parts above the voice box, and be convinced of the necessity of a perfectly controlled chest expansion in the production of tone.

For perfect singing, correct breathing, strange as it may sound, is even more essential than a beautiful voice. No matter how exquisite the vocal organ may be, its beauty cannot be adequately demonstrated without proper breath control. Here is one of the old Italian secrets which many singers of to-day wholly lack, because they are unwilling to give the necessary time for the full development of breathing power and control. Phrasing, tone, resonance, expression, all depend upon respiration; and in my opinion musical students, even when too young to be allowed the free use of the voice, should be thoroughly taught the principles of breathing.

Indeed, the science of taking breath is a study peculiarly suited to the years of childhood and adolescence; for apart from other considerations, there are few things so conducive to good health as good breathing. And, owing to the greater elasticity of the human frame in the time of youth, the chest is then more easily developed and expanded.

Any exercises that give strength to the diaphragm are of special value, since this is the principal muscle of inspiration. Expiration, however, is not so easily controlled as inspiration, and on that score calls for the most careful practice. Faulty or hurried breathing always interferes with the true vibration of the vocal strands, and all circumstances that tend toward either should be scrupulously avoided; more especially at the time of a singer's first entrance on the stage or concert platform, which is always a moment of nervousness and doubt.

It is an excellent practice for a nervous singer to take a few deep breaths on entering, and the inexperienced should avoid numbers with exacting opening bars.

Few people, by the way, realise how much even the most famous of singers is at the mercy of the audience, and how a wave of indifference or apathy borne from the serried thousands of a theatre or concert-hall can often take all the colour out of the loveliest voice, and all the necessary abandon out of an interpretation. I have known some of the greatest singers of our day—and myself, too—to fall incredibly below their normal standard for no other reason than that of irresponsiveness on the part of their audience. In this respect I confess I am myself extremely sensitive. I can almost always give my best when I feel that the heart of the audience bids me excel.

Even a good general knowledge of music does not imply knowledge of scientific voice production. Correct vocalisation is only possible on strict physiological principles. I insist upon this, because it is rational and logical. In this way faults are better recognised and explained; the student may the more surely guide her own development or effectively restore an injured voice, and generally advance her physical welfare, which is a vital point.

Therefore those who do not believe in attainment through patient and intelligent labour would do well to abandon an art career, for that way lies disappointment. "Hasten slowly" applies supremely in the highest voice culture; but, unhappily, this is not the note of our age.

According to my idea, the student of singing can best learn this subtle and complex art in those centres where music has been longest established and most generally practised; where it is, in a word, part of the daily life of the people rather than the recreation or luxury of the few. For this reason I consistently recommend study in Italy, France, and Germany, and particularly for American, Canadian, English, and Australian students. I put my own country last, in the spirit of courtesy; but as a producer of voices it really ought to come first in consideration.

As I have said, I am opposed to every girl with a little knowledge of music embracing the art as a profession merely because she considers it more "genteel" than other avenues to earning a livelihood. A girl should have some real qualification before she looks forward to becoming a professional singer. Kindly and necessarily biassed compliments from relatives and friends on the singing of a few ballads in the home-circle or at an amateur concert should not be sufficient to thrust her upon the patience of the musical public. High and unprejudiced authority should be sought for her guidance, preferably from a singer who knows the conditions and atmosphere of the world's greatest musical centres.

In this regard a person who has had only local experience cannot possibly be a good judge of what is needed for the career of a great singer. An invaluable factor in musical success is the study of foreign languages. These are always most successfully acquired in the countries where they are the native tongue.

Thus, residence in the established centres of music in the Old World and intimacy with their language and traditions give the student a surety and authority in her work that cannot possibly be gained in any other way. Of course, robust physical health is of paramount importance. Without it a great vocal career is absolutely barred.

I admit that there is much in a singer's life conducive to this physical robustness; as, for example, the vigorous use of the breathing apparatus. But this may be more than counteracted by late hours, much travelling by night, concentrated efforts, and disappointment resulting from the caprice of public taste or other causes. Plenty of fresh air, plain food, a reasonable amount of exercise, and eight or nine hours' sleep are all necessary to the young singer, whose larynx is quick to reflect the general physical condition.

At the same time, common sense and individual temperament should be the best of all health rules. I myself always suffer in a steam-heated apartment; I consider the general overheating in America a menace, and never allow the temperature of my rooms to rise above 60 degrees; while at the same time the whole range of my apartments is continually freshened with pure air.

The singer should aim at becoming a hardy plant rather than a hot-house flower. I know that a girl with a voice receives a painful revelation of the delicacy of her vocal organs when she passes from a superheated room to the low temperature of a winter's day outside. But I consider dry feet far more important than the muffling up of the throat on raw, slushy days

A singer's diet should include plenty of fresh fruit and vegetables. I myself take for breakfast only a cup of tea and a little toast. At luncheon I have a cutlet or a little chicken, some stewed fruit, with a light salad, but no rich food. My chief meal is, of course, dinner, which I take rather late at night, generally at 7.45, unless I am singing, when I take a light—very light—meal about five in the afternoon.

A question often asked me is, "How early should a girl begin the more serious business of voice culture?" Never before she is seventeen. Even a limited study before that age will interfere with the development of the vocal organs, and perhaps do them serious injury. Among my daily letters are many from girls of fifteen and sixteen asking for a hearing; but I always tell them they are too young, however promising. As to the age limit the other way, I feel it would be impossible to give any good general advice.

I would point out, in this connection, that some artists of world-wide repute are singing as well today as they did twenty years ago, while others have broken down in a few short years, or have become hopelessly defective in their vocal results. It is all a question of correct or incorrect methods.

Apropos of the need for foreign languages, I recall an amusing episode. Not long after my début in Brussels as Gilda in "Rigoletto," I began to study the opera of "Lakmé" under the direction of Delibes, its composer. But my pronunciation of French at that time was evidently considered by the directors of the opera as the French of Stratford-atte-Bowe, and they doubted whether I ought to sing in "Lakmé" at all. One day, much perplexed in council, they sent for the composer, and told him their troubles. "Qu'elle chante en chinois, si elle veut," cried Delibes, pounding the table with angry fist, "mais qu'elle chante mon opéra!" ("She may sing in Chinese if she likes, so long as she sings my opera.") But I was really backward in French, and on that account set to work and studied no less than six hours a day under a thoroughly competent Brussels teacher.

At the same time, I should warn the student to be careful not to overdo her work, in her enthusiasm for all the musical advantages she sees about her. I think music should be thoroughly known before it is sung. It is a serious tax on the voice to sit down at the piano and try to sing an aria with which the singer is not familiar. Half an hour's practice is enough, unless the student has exceptional physique; in that case I should say half an hour every morning and afternoon.

I have met scores of students abroad whose mistaken diligence impels them to practise for hours at a stretch. Such an error may do irretrievable harm to a voice. It is well to realise that the entire vocal mechanism is an exquisitely delicate instrument, capable of being played upon by its owner in a way almost impersonal, so that ignorance may mean fatal injury. For this reason no enthusiasm would induce practice to the extent of tiring the voice.

As to how long this foreign study should last, this, of course, depends upon the mental capacity of the student. Young singers of many nations cite to me my own case; for after nine months' study in Paris, I came out as a full-fledged prima donna at the Brussels Opera House. But I may say at once that mine was an exceptional case, for I was born with a natural trill and an absolute control of breath, so that as a child of seven I was as far advanced naturally as some mature students are after years of patient study.

In connection with the natural trill, my fellow-pupils at college in East Melbourne, Australia, used to gather round me and say curiously, "Nellie, make that funny noise in your throat." It amused them. But to assume that the *bel canto* of perfect technique is to be acquired after nine months' foreign study would be unwise. On the other hand, as I have already stated, if a girl cannot give good account of herself after eighteen months' serious study, I think she is not destined to illuminate vocal art.

Still, any ordinary term spent in vocal study cannot be regarded as wasted, for no system of physical exercise is so beneficial to a woman as that involved in the higher branches of vocal culture. At least the disappointed one carries back with her a pleasing and expressive voice for ordinary conversation. Here is a matter to which little attention is paid, yet how much pleasure does a beautiful speaking voice convey! It is surely a valuable asset all through life.

As to extraneous aids to vocal study, there is none so beneficial as the constant hearing of great singers in the roles which have secured them fame. Indeed, no matter what branch of music a girl selects for her special study, I should strongly urge her to hear all the fine music possible, whether opera, orchestra, concert, or oratorio. She can learn something valuable from all. Let me emphasise this point, for in this way the student will see theory put into practice. It is as if a young painter should visit the marvellous Tribuna of the Uffizi Palace in Florence, where the supreme examples of the great masters are hung; or the young sculptor should study Michel Angelo in the vast galleries of the Vatican. Thus no opportunity of hearing accepted interpreters should be lost.

The student who goes to Europe, of course, has exceptional opportunities all the year round; but the American or English girl can hear in New York or London during the musical season a combination of singers, conductors, and instrumentalists that is the best of the entire musical world

In addition, she should read everything authoritative on music and musicians, at the same time *not* confining herself to musical subjects. For a wide and wise reading of everything that broadens the mind and gives one a truer knowledge of art and nature is of supreme importance. Nothing so helps the interpretative sense as a fine and cultivated imagination, and an appreciation of nature's beauties, great paintings, statuary, and the best literature gives one an artistic grasp not possible to the student who is merely well informed on musical matters.

While I am a strong advocate of foreign study, I think it a pity that so many American and British students elect to swell permanently the over-crowded ranks of the musical profession on the continent of Europe instead of returning to the less crowded centres of their home lands, and giving their compatriots the benefit of their experience and example. It is given to few of us to attain world prominence, and those to whom such fame is manifestly impossible should not fear to try for the best their own country offers, which may be a great and dignified meed.

Adequate study in Europe requires a good deal of money. For most young girls a chaperon or companion is essential; although there are a number of places where a solitary young student may find the comfort and the protection of a home. Where this is possible the expenses are naturally much less.

The leading professors on the Continent charge from a guinea to two guineas a lesson, with a certain reduction of an extended term. Three lessons a week are usual. As to the expenses of living, even on the most moderate scale they cannot be reasonably estimated at less than five guineas a week for board, dress, allowance, concert and opera tickets, and general expenses. This, with lessons extending over eighteen months or more, runs into a considerable sum.

To the student with wealth as well as voice the way would appear smooth; yet I would offer a word of warning. First, the flattery of friends and possibly unscrupulous advisers is dangerous. Besides, the fact of affluence tends to diminish the sense of responsibility. Money, it must be borne in mind, cannot buy purity of tone, temperament, or correct breathing. These entail hard work, even with natural gifts. One cannot buy brains with money, or even the ability to appreciate the brains of others, and the loveliest voice that ever charmed the world must be guided and used through the intellect; otherwise it must fall far short of the highest standard.

The point is that a wealthy student may become slack, and forget how wide must be the culture of a great singer. A complete study of piano, counterpoint, and harmony are as necessary as grammar to the spoken language; and all that is best in this big, busy world must be seized upon and brought into service, for divine music is an exigent goddess.

The poor student with an exceptional voice is unfortunately placed, and advice to her must be of a negative kind. She may fall into the mistake of thinking that if she can get into choir or chorus she will be advancing to some extent. But while a well-trained voice may be used in a chorus without serious harm, the girl who knows nothing about placing her voice, and is prodigal in the use of it, may find chorus work most injurious.

Many ambitious young women save money with the aim of attending a musical college. This is an education I never advocate, for I believe in individual training. No student can attain the best results in a class where personal supervision is a matter of perfunctory duty. Certainly good singers have come from musical colleges, but they have had temperament and personality such as rise above the system. And to work at any trade or profession while cultivating the voice is a questionable arrangement, for the student takes vitality from the voice and places it in another direction.

I doubt if one could with correctness summarily assign characteristics to the vocal students of the different nations; and, besides, one likes to think of music as cosmopolitan—universal in its inspiration and influence. The Italian girl is perhaps the readiest to help her song by facial expression, the French girl the first to master the poetic message, and the German the most thorough in all-round pursuit of musical knowledge. Many American and British students are too easily satisfied, and often, on securing a certain measure of success at their first public appearance, refrain from further study at the very time that their work should be regarded as beginning in real earnest.

As to the voices of the different nations with which I am familiar, it is a difficult and thankless task to summarise them within the inadequate limit of a few lines. I should say, however, that the voices of Italy are the most natural. They are the voices of the sun; just as in my native land, Australia, the Italy of the southern hemisphere, the voices seem to glint and vibrate as it with liquid sunlight. There is in these Southern voices a resonance rarely found in voices of the North.

As to Germany, I should say that the singing voices are more the result of science than of nature—less buoyant, less responsive, yet superb in their own way. The great singers of France, to my mind, could be more accurately described as great *diseurs*, so exquisitely are they practised in the art of diction. No singers so effectively show the beauty or importance of the words sung.

The cosmopolitan conditions of America seem to me to have so far militated against the development of any particular voice or school that could be accurately labelled "American," while the English voices are particularly adapted for concert and oratorio singing.

Owing to the characteristic reserve of the English people, they are, as a rule, slow to commit themselves to that temperamental abandon which is essential to operatic interpretation. I am, however, glad to be able to say without any reserve that I consider the English choruses the finest in the world. I refer more specially to the great choirs heard at the English musical festivals. What volume and beauty of tone, what precision and light and shade, are embodied in their work! Personally, if I can be said to dislike any form of music, it is oratorio; but when I hear an English chorus at a festival in Birmingham, Leeds, Bristol, or Worcester, I am almost persuaded to become an oratorio enthusiast.

This paper would not be complete without some reference to personal appearance as an asset in a singer's career. There is much suggestion, expression even, in the turn of a curl. The woman who knows how to "make up" effectively is more of an artist than the one who does not. The whole thing makes for artistic completeness.

I have known handsome women appear unattractive on the stage or platform merely because they relied entirely on their natural physical gifts without considering how these were affected by the space, and structural and lighting conditions, of the building in which they sang. There are cases where good looks are the main reason for the exploitation of a singer; but such favour is bound to be short-lived, and no artistic reputation can be long maintained on so false a basis.

As to securing an introduction to the public, I have little to say beyond the fact that ability will surely find its way. In my own path great obstacles were placed, but I do not think anything in this world could have hindered me from becoming a singer. I have sung to an audience of two, and such was my girlish enthusiasm that I have even acted as my own billposter, with a pot of paste procured from a hotel kitchen. The occasion was a chanty concert at an Australian seaside resort for the purpose of repairing a neglected country cemetery. Later I had to abandon proposed concerts because there was not enough support to pay for the lighting of the hall. Yet I persevered, and my chance came. It is well to aim at the highest, yet in my heart of hearts I believe that every really great singer is born rather than made.

No teacher living can impart temperament and an infallible ear for music. A perfect chest, larynx, and resonance chambers are also gifts of God; and so, too, are the musical intuition, the ravishing voice, the industry, the ambition, and the perfect physical health, which are all attributes of vocalists who have become really great.

But below that heavenly gifted circle there are many niches which should be filled, not by casual observers, but by qualified musicians, to whom hard and patient work has brought attainments second only to those fortunate creatures who have sprung into the musical arena, like Minerva, fully equipped.

past a doubt, young singers can learn much about the highest ar ltivation of the voice from watching the knowledge of technique o operatic artists, and from observing their methods of "managing" . Still, to thoroughly grasp the progress of the opera-singer's art, necessary for students to appreciate the fact that Italian singing two important culminating periods, each of which was illustrated up of great singers, the first of which was made up of pupils o i, Pistocchi, Francesca Cuzzoni, and other contemporary teachers. eat singers brought the art of *bel canto* to as near a state of perfection ver been known. But one has to remember the conditions under ey sang.

s Victor Maurel writes:—"In the days of the schools of the art of *bel* masters did not have to take truth for expression (*l'expression juste*) ount, for the singer was not required to render the sentiments of *atis personæ* with verisimilitude; all that was demanded of him was ous sounds, the *bel canto*." In other words, all that the singer had s to sing, for the emotions themselves had not to be portrayed, the l character of the *dramatis personæ* not being taken into account.

onsequence, the perfection of the singer's voice was but slightly d with, as, at most, he had little or no acting to do, a conventional l gesture or two being considered quite sufficient for the fashion riod. And it is scarcely necessary to remark that the great singers eriod were skilful enough musicians to prevent such unimportant , which hardly deserve the dignity of the name of acting, from being cle to the high quality of their singing.

ne second period of Italian singing, however, the period which s with the Rossini-Donizetti-Bellini period of opera in its heydey, litions, we find, were greatly altered. The music at this time was more dramatic and more scenic, and although the singing was *anto*, the opera singer of the period was called upon not only to sing t to sing dramatically, though it must be said that the music itself d larger scope for the actor's art, in that it gave more favourable nity for specialising and differentiating the emotions.

The Opera Past and Present" we find the following intensely ng allusion to these two great culminating periods of Italian —"A comparison of these two periods of Italian singing indicates ction matters have taken with the opera singer from Handel's our own. From then to now he has had to face an ever-increasing ation of untoward conditions; his professional work has become d more complicated. From Rossini's time down to this the purely

HINTS ON THE CULTIVATION OF THE VOICE By ENRICO CARUSO

It has often struck me, in a lengthy experience as a singer, that there is one point in particular about the human voice which is far too little appreciated by the rising generation of aspiring vocalists, and that is its wonderful reciprocity. Tend it, nurse it, "feed it on a proper diet," and it will invariably comport itself in the most amiable manner possible. But neglect it, treat it as an organ which is best left to look after itself, and the voice will at once, in revenge for this callous behaviour, retaliate by behaving itself in a manner which is perhaps best described as of the "hooliganistic" order.

And yet, as an actual fact, but a very small percentage indeed of would-be singers ever really seem to think it worth their while to bear in mind this axiom, for axiom it surely is, that the voice requires proper care and proper exercise to keep it in its best form just as much as is a certain amount of exercise necessary to the maintenance of good health in every human being.

Unfortunately, however, there would seem to be a prevalent impression among many amateur and not a few professional singers that singing is an art which can be acquired in quite a short time. Thus, is it not curious that while many students of the piano or the violin will willingly devote years of strenuous and conscientious practice to the study of the technique of these instruments, would-be singers frequently seem to expect to learn how to use their voice to the best advantage after a period of vocal practice extending, maybe, over a year or so, but more often even over only a few months? This policy, I need scarcely remark, is absolutely ruinous to the future careers of young singers, for no matter how naturally talented any individual vocalist may be, he or she cannot possibly produce the best results as a singer unless the particular organs brought into play in the process of singing have been subjected to a proper and sufficiently long course of training. Since the days of the old Italian masters there can be no shadow of doubt that, musically, we have advanced considerably; but sometimes, when I think of the rather slipshod methods of cultivating the voice advocated by many so-called "professors" to-day, the thought impresses itself on my mind that the detailed principles of the old Italian masters who, above all other considerations, insisted on a long course of voice training as being the only possible means to the attainment of the best art, possessed more to recommend them than do many of the modern "artifices" of voice-cultivation proffered by many teachers of singing to-day.

In a short article, of course, it is obviously impossible to go in detail into all the rules which should be observed by singers who are prepared to undertake the task of cultivating their voices on a conscientious and sound basis. At the same time, I hope to be able to suggest various hints and wrinkles which should prove of real value to aspiring singers.

In the first place, therefore, let me say at once that it is the most fatal of all errors for a singer to make too much use of the voice, for the muscles of the larynx are so delicate that they cannot possibly stand the strain of the "learn-to-sing-in-a-hurry" methods of those who hope to attain the highest point of proficiency without devoting sufficient time to that "drudgery" which is absolutely essential to the real and perfect cultivation of the voice.

For this all-important reason I would counsel singers to see to it at all times that in the early days of their training they do not devote too much time to practice. If they will take my advice, until they become thoroughly proficient in "managing" the voice—a happy state of affairs which can only be acquired after long practice—they will at first never devote more than fifteen minutes a day—in the early morning is, perhaps, the best time—to practice. I can readily realise that this must seem a very short time to enthusiasts who are willing to give up all their spare time to the study of voice cultivation, but it is, nevertheless, quite long enough, for the slightest strain put upon the voice may retard a singer's progress by months, while, on the other hand, as I pointed out at the beginning of this article, if the singer will only bear in mind that the voice requires the most careful "nursing" of perhaps all the organs, and must on no account be strained, he will soon find that, though he may not be aware of any improvement in it, his voice is, nevertheless, slowly but surely improving and gaining in strength through his gradually-growing knowledge of technique.

Another point in the cultivation of the voice which I often think is not sufficiently strongly emphasised to-day is the fact that young singers can improve their methods in the most extraordinarily rapid manner by studying the methods of other and more experienced singers. In singing, as in the cultivation of the other arts, in time the student will get what he works for, but it is surely unreasonable for him to expect to sing effectively by his own inspiration. He will be wise, therefore, to seize every opportunity of studying as closely as possible the methods of those who have thoroughly mastered the technique of singing. For true art, of course, there must be more than technique, but I would point out that in singing there is no art

without sound methods of execution, which, afte
purposes constitute technique. In the cultivation o
and sympathy in the voice, there is no better teac
opera." Still, I make no doubt that of the hundreds
visit the opera during the season but very few in
through the years of drudgery as conscientiously a
to sing so easily and to combine the art of acting a
time with equal facility. After all, the highest art
of that art, and I take it that it is because a really
accomplishes his performance with such apparent
of operatic singing are so little appreciated.

Still, as I have said, I am strongly of the opinion
learn much from studying the methods of operatic
when they have mastered the rudiments of voice
need not enter here, for my object is rather to show
by which they can attain the highest art when they
apprenticeship under masters whose duty it is to te
rules of singing.

For my own part, I find that a singer's life, wit
and performances, is such a busy one that not much
him for indulging in outdoor exercise. Many ot
doubtless find themselves situated in very similar
account of their public engagements, but through
their time by business, social, or domestic duties.
voice, however, a certain amount of exercise is ess
by the same token, is good health a *sine quâ non*
highest art in singing. It may be of service, therefor
observe when I find the calls upon my time too nu
get as much exercise as I should otherwise like.

No matter how busy I am, when I rise in the mor
in a few simple physical exercises, similar in char
practise when, as a young man, the time came for m
country as a *soldato*, or, if I feel that these are beco
few minutes I find practice with a pair of dumb-b
the way—very beneficial. But save these mild for
as a rule, to rest content with, in the way of outdoo
motor drive. Nevertheless, I would point out that, i
constant deep inhalation, is by no means inconsid
to be sure, I am well aware that it cannot be so heal
actual exercise in the open air.

musical difficulties he has had to face have been constantly on the increase—complexity of musical structure, rhythmic complications, hazardous intonations.

"He has to fight against the more and more brilliant style of instrumentation, often pushed to a point where the greatest stress of vocal effort is required of him to make himself heard above the orchestral din; more and better acting is demanded of him, he finds the vague generalities of histrionism no longer of avail; for these must make way for a highly specialised, real-seeming dramatic impersonation; intellectually and physically his task has been doubled and trebled. Above all, the sheer nervous tension of situations and music has so increased as to make due self-control on his part less easy. The opera singer's position to-day is verily no joke; he has to face and conquer difficulties such as the great *bel cantists* of the Handel period never dreamt of."

It has ever been my contention that the conscientious artist should carefully read and re-read the whole libretto, so as to inform himself of the poet's purpose and meaning in the construction and development of the plot, as well as to ever bear in mind his conception of the composer's idea of how the poetry and the various aspects of mind of the characters should be aptly and effectively musicked and interpreted so as to awaken a kindred, or appreciative, feeling in the minds of his hearers.

Besides this, the opera singer who aspires to rise to great heights must possess a keen nervous susceptibility, for only a man or woman of high nervous temperament can reasonably hope to succeed as a lyrico-dramatic artist. Again, in the great operas a most severe strain is placed upon the leading singers, for while they are portraying various emotions—-Love, Hate, Rage, or Laughter—they have, at the same time, to watch the conductor with most minute care lest they fail in time and rhythm.

In fine, though I think but few other than really conscientious students of singing entirely appreciate the fact, the opera-singer of to-day is called upon to possess a far greater knowledge of vocal technique than was ever demanded of him before in the history of singing, as those "good and golden days"—golden only to the moderate performer with but little ambition—when the singer who perhaps scarcely knew more than a few notes of music could, nevertheless, still arouse the plaudits of the public are gone—never to return.

I hope, by the way, that it will not be thought that I have entered too technically into the requirements demanded from an aspirant to operatic fame to-day. I scarcely think, however, that I can have done so, for I feel sure every really aspiring vocalist would prefer to know the exact heights to which he must cultivate his voice either on the operatic stage or concert platform, or even for the drawing-room, that is to say, if he is ever to make a great name for himself in preference to resting content to remain one of the "moderates," of which the musical profession is altogether already too full, not because there is a lack of singers with good voices, but largely, as I have always maintained, because there is a far too prevalent tendency amongst singers these days to shirk the real hard work which must be accomplished before lasting success can be attained.

In conclusion, in order to allow singers' voices to develop in a satisfactory manner, let me counsel them never to attempt those selections in public the range of which taxes and strains them to the utmost, for when a singer "exceeds" his proper range injury to the throat is always liable to follow. Better rather, therefore, is it that a song should be transposed to a lower key if a singer is determined to attempt it than that the voice should be unduly taxed.

And now I will say *addio*, though I would add that it is my sincere hope that some of the few hints I have given on the cultivation of the voice and of the heights of excellence to which ambitious singers should aspire may prove of real value to those with sufficient pluck to face the task of studying the art of the cultivation of the voice in a really conscientious manner. Hard work accomplishes wonders where the voice is concerned. Let me, therefore, counsel singers never to despair of attaining a state as near to perfection as possible, for it is those who are most alive to their own imperfections who will assuredly "go farthest" in the singing world.

HOW TO ATTAIN SUCCESS IN SINGING By BEN DAVIES

To a certain extent it must be admitted at once that it is undoubtedly true that there is no royal, infallible road to success in the acquirement of perfect mastery over any art. At the same time, however, I would lay particular stress on the fact that it is equally true that there are not a few hints and wrinkles which, if studiously borne in mind and practised, must inevitably prove of real value to all who will apply themselves to these said words of advice in a thoroughly whole-hearted manner.

And, in particular, this somewhat trite aphorism applies with great force to the art of learning to sing, for the human voice, as every conscientious student of music must be well aware, is an exceptionally responsive organ. Neglect it, and it will assuredly "run to seed"; tend it carefully, cultivate it in a common-sense manner, give it time to "grow up," and it will reward you for your pains a hundredfold.

Let me, therefore, try and give a few hints based on an experience extending over more years than I sometimes care to think about, which I trust will prove of real value to aspiring singers. I have already said that there is no royal road to success in the art of learning to sing, but, nevertheless, the possessor of a moderate voice can improve his or her voice in a most gratifying manner by studying in the right way. Bad habits in singing are peculiarly difficult to rid oneself of; it is well to avoid the risk of acquiring those bad habits by setting out on the right road at once. And having started, push forward with unfailing energy and courage.

In the first place I would counsel the ambitious singer, before proceeding with the development of the voice to ascertain its real character and quality. Thus, some voices, to the ear of the trained expert, although they may be actually untrained and undeveloped, nevertheless possess a decided and marked quality when still uncultivated, while, on the other hand, there are other voices whose positive nature it is far from easy to determine. I would therefore emphasise the fact that it is not upon its range and extent that the real character of any individual voice depends, but rather upon its quality and timbre.

I would lay stress, too, on another point—namely, that the real power of expression is found in the middle quality of every voice, and that it is not force which tends to make this middle quality full and resonant, but the cultivated ease and steadiness by which the vocal sounds are produced and sustained. There is nothing more painful to the ear of an expert musician than to hear a singer forcing his voice in an effort to produce an effect of expansion and vibration. Would-be artistic singers should thus nurse their voices with unfailing care, for ease and steadiness are infinitely more artistic than forcing the voice.

I will not here enter into the question of what particular exercises the student should follow in his or her early days, for such matters are too elementary a kind and can safely be trusted to any competent teacher. At the same time I would point out that the careful vocal student will be wise to adopt the style of music best adapted to his or her voice, for, obvious though this point should be, it is none the less true that many singers overlook the fact that to give the voice an adequate chance of developing it should be cultivated and "fed" upon the particular style of music for which Nature would seem to have given it birth.

Again, I am taking it for granted that the singer has safely weathered the storms inseparable from the initial or drudgery side of voice cultivation—particular care should be exercised in the selection of songs, for I have frequently noted that many singers who should surely have known better, have, nevertheless, frequently failed to give their voices a chance of showing their real merit by selecting songs utterly unsuited to them. Thus, maybe, a male singer has gone out of his way to select a song especially intended for a lady, while the latter has shown a pronounced predilection for singing songs intended solely for men. The result of such an unwise selection is surely best left to the imagination.

And now let me say a few words about the manner in which students should study their musical compositions. Almost every singer possibly possesses some small peculiarity in this respect, but I think I cannot do better than quote the system of study followed out by those two great artists, Grisi and Mario; for, frankly, to a great extent their methods may, among future generations, well become "standard methods."

"In studying any new composition, whether the most important opera, or the simplest ballad, they followed a set plan. It was this: the words were first considered, and when the intention and meaning of the text had been clearly ascertained and fully understood, then, and not till then, the music with which it was associated, was learnt by heart—every salient feature and opportunity for effect being most carefully thought over and decided upon."

"It was one of Mario's maxims, that unless a singer had all he was singing about thoroughly in his head, as well as in his throat, he could never do himself justice."

"'But,' he used to say, 'if you get as familiar as you should be with your work, then, when you are in the humour, and in good voice, you can let yourself go, with the certainty almost of producing the effect you intend upon your audience—that is to say, if you ever have any moments of inspiration.'"

"Whether in considering the dramatic effects to be made by 'Raoul and Valentina,' or in taking in hand 'Good-bye, Sweetheart,' or 'The Minstrel Boy,' the plan they followed was the same. The words were thought of first, then the music, and, with the words and music combined, particular attention was given to the points to be dwelt on and made prominent. These latter were not allowed to be too frequent, but were so chosen as to make the deepest impression."

"The importance of such a plan as this can hardly be overrated. It seems not only to ensure singing with intelligence, but to save a singer very much unnecessary exertion, by marking down the intervals where energy has to be used, as well as those where the voice may, so to speak, be nursed and kept in reserve."

Speaking of a pianoforte accompaniment, Mario used to say, "The art of accompanying is displayed in the following, aiding, and supporting the singer; not in hurrying him, nor in drowning his voice."

An accompanist, in his opinion, should never be timid; but, if uncertain of the notes to be played, should, nevertheless, strike them firmly and courageously, otherwise the singer gets confused, loses confidence in himself and the accompaniment, and the effect intended to be produced suffers irretrievably in consequence.

I would commend a study of this system to the aspiring singer, with every confidence that, if he follows out the said methods, he will be assuredly pursuing a policy than which there can be few better.

It may not now be out of place if I say a few words on the act of production of the voice. Many beginners thus make the mistake of imagining that to give the voice a proper chance of expanding to the full it is necessary that the mouth should be opened wide in the act of singing.

This, however, is quite an erroneous idea, for, as a matter of actual, hard fact, the mouth should not be too open when the act of singing is taking place, though I would point out that when it is opening the jaws should be allowed to fall in a natural manner—in other words, by their own weight—

while, if the lips are, at the same time, pressed gently against the teeth, the mouth naturally assumes a pleasant form. There is nothing more appalling than to watch a singer indulging in exaggerated facial contortions which may perhaps impress a musical tyro as "imposing," but which, nevertheless, are actually more often than not nothing but a species of absurd affectation.

The management of the breath, of course, is to a great extent a distinct and separate study in singing, though I may perhaps be allowed to say that absolute control of the breath is a *sine quâ non* to perfect enunciation. It will be well, therefore, for every really ambitious singer to see to it that his or her master possesses a thoroughly sound knowledge of managing the breath; otherwise, all too early in their careers, they may acquire habits which they will find extremely difficult to break, for experience has taught me that, as far as singing is concerned, bad habits are possessed of unpleasantly tenacious qualities.

As far as the position of the body in singing is concerned, the old-time rule that the shoulders should be thrown back firmly and naturally is as "in order" to-day as it was thirty years ago, while that the chest should be steadily and not hurriedly expanded is also an equally sound policy to pursue. Manual Garcia recommended the following exercises as of great value in increasing the power and elasticity of the lungs. I make no apology for quoting these, as they cannot fail to prove worth diligent study, though, especially at first, they will be found distinctly exhausting, for which reason young singers should make a point of practising each exercise separately.

Gently and slowly inhale for a few seconds as much air as the chest will contain.

After taking a deep breath, exhale again very gently and slowly.

Fill the lungs, and keep them inflated for the longest possible time.

Exhale completely, and leave the chest empty as long as physical powers will conveniently allow.

In a short article it is obviously impossible for me to go as deeply into the art of voice production as I should like, though there is one "aspect" of singing on which I would lay great stress—and that is the value of colour in singing.

In a study of all the great composers and their works, to the true student of music, it must be patent at once that their methods of colouring vary as greatly as do the *chefs-d'oeuvre* of masters of the brush.

And yet, somehow or other, I do not think that I am wandering away from the straight road of Truth when I say that, as a general rule, the mediocre singer but seldom realises that there is such a thing as colour in singing. What is the result? It is the natural result of cause and effect. The interpretation of the ordinary singer resembles to no small extent the work of an artist who sketches out an outline drawing which, in detail, no doubt is accurate and thoroughly praiseworthy in every way; but when compared to a painting with its appealing richness of tone and colour it seems a puny thing indeed.

Yes, it is colour that the average singer utterly lacks. But let me hasten to say at once that for this sin of omission he or she, as the case may be, merits no real discredit, for the simple reason that those who have only limited time to devote to the study of singing naturally find that their training does not, as a rule, reach the point when they are sufficiently able exponents to be able to paint pictures with their voices, much in the same way as does the artist paint his pictures on canvas. And in no small measure this sin of omission is as much due to the methods of instruction of the teacher as it is to the pupil's lack of advancement.

Yes, there can be no doubt that it is through lack of study of these "finer" details in the art of singing which causes many vocalists never to rise above the mediocre. Technically, they may be thoroughly capable exponents, but unless they realise the incalculable value of tone and colour in music, they fail to extract from it its real poetical worth. Thus, when listening to Schumann—to revert to pianoforte playing for a moment—"they fail to wander hand in hand with the composer into some glorious garden full of gaily-coloured flowers, through trim paths lined by tall, stately trees. They fail to see in Schumann's music gaily-plumaged birds flitting here and there beneath a blue sky with the warm rays of the sun toning everything into summer as if by fairy hand."

It was an ardent student of pianoforte playing who once thus described to me a composition of Schumann's as played by a real master. And with singing it is much the same. For some curious reason your moderate singer will persist in cherishing an utterly erroneous notion that every song should be "treated" in one way—in other words, that when framing his composition, the composer mentally decreed that, to be rendered as he intended it should be, every singer must sink his individuality and render it in one way—and one way only.

Was ever notion more unreasonable? Surely it is the most glaring error possible to imagine that because a melody is simple, because it can be rendered by the average singer after but comparatively little practice, it must be impossible to imbue it with beautiful effects; for no matter how technically simple a composition may be, provided a singer possesses real soul and a sense of poetry he or she can bring out an exquisite beauty and colour from the music which a mere mechanical vocalist who merely regards a simple piece as an easy piece to sing invariably fails to recognise.

It is the thoughtless and mechanical practice of a really musical subject which undermines the musical sense, for the practice of purely mechanical matter should never be "dry" so long as the singer thoroughly grasps the real objects to be attained from that practice. In other words, every exercise, every piece of music that is sung, ought to be rendered with a clearly-defined object. It seems to me that one of the most powerful reasons why the results of years of study are so often unsatisfactory lies in the fact that many singers are far too early occupied with the study of compositions of every sort, adding continually to their stock without devoting sufficient time to the introspective study of each and every piece.

What is the inevitable outcome of this hasty and wholesale method of "learning to sing"? Interpretations which, as I have said, are like outline drawing, accurate enough in detail but comparatively lacking in real soul and wanting altogether in tone and colour. I admit at once, as among artists we all have our favourites, so among song-writers the works of some appeal to us more than do others, in that we respond to one or other of them more readily than to the rest. But, at the same time, I would lay special emphasis on the fact that every song, however simple, should be dealt with by the singer like a separate picture in which specially beautiful effects may be produced, according to the quality and variety of tone and colour.

And not until singers realise that the composition is but the raw material waiting to be imbued with expression at their hands, waiting, in fine, to be given life, personality, and real being, can they thoroughly grasp the innermost meaning of music which, rendered by the true artist, expresses more clearly than any words ever written, the true emotions of the soul.